Attach a picture of your baby in the frame above

This Keepsake Book of Faith Moments
is presented to

_____

by

_____

Wonderfully Made!

A Keepsake Book of Faith Moments

Wonderfully Made!
A Keepsake Book of Faith Moments

WONDERFULLY MADE!
A Keepsake Book of Faith Moments

Large-quantity purchases of this book are available at a discount from the publisher. For more information, contact the sales department at Augsburg Fortress, Publishers, 1-800-328-4648, or write to: Sales Director, Augsburg Fortress, Publishers, Box 1209, Minneapolis, MN 55440-1209.

Scripture passages, unless otherwise marked, are from the New Revised Standard Version of the Bible, copyright © 1946, 1952, 1971, 1989 by the Division of Christian Education of the National Council of the Churches of Christ in the USA. Used by permission.

Scripture passages marked NIV are from the Holy Bible, New International Version, copyright © 1973, 1978, 1984 International Bible Society. Used by permission of Zondervan Publishing House. All rights reserved.

ISBN-13: 978-0-8066-5320-4
ISBN-10: 0-8066-5320-5

Written by Kristin Limberg and Tera Michelson
Edited by Dawn Rundman and Michelle L. N. Cook
Illustrated by Mary Jo Scandin
Cover designed by Diana Running
Book designed by Michelle L. N. Cook

The paper used in this publication meets the minimum requirements of American National Standard for Information Sciences—Permanence of Paper for Printed Library Materials, ANSI Z329.48-1984.

Manufactured in Peru.

10   09   08   07   2   3   4   5   6   7   8   9   10

Welcome to your wondrous new role as parent to a precious child of God! The title of this keepsake book, *Wonderfully Made!,* is based on Psalm 139:13-14: "For it was you who formed my inward parts; you knit me together in my mother's womb. I praise you, for I am fearfully and wonderfully made."

As you begin the journey of parenthood with your wonderfully made baby, we hope you find this beautifully illustrated keepsake book valuable. Our writers, Kristin Limberg and Tera Michelson, have filled its pages with thoughtful content and plenty of places to write about and reflect on your child's faith during his or her first three years.

Some of this book's topics refer to specific events like baptism, birthdays, and holidays. Other pages can be revisited many times during your child's first three years. Leaf through the pages now to get an idea of its contents. Then keep *Wonderfully Made!* in an accessible place so you can easily jot down thoughts, add photos, and record memories. You could even ask guest writers (grandparent, godparent, close friend) to add their views to some of the pages.

God—who formed your child's inward parts—knows your child deeply and intimately. Your child's faith formation has already begun! *Wonderfully Made!* will help you remember joys and insights along the way as she or he continues this lifelong journey in the presence of family, friends, godparents, congregation members, and other faithful ones.

May God bless your family of faith!

Dawn Rundman

Dawn Rundman, Ph.D.
Lead Editor of Splash! resources

Baby

Mother

Father

Grandmother

Grandfather

Grandmother

Grandfather

Other family members (siblings, aunts, uncles, cousins)

_____

_____

_____

_____

_____

Great Grandparents (write each one's name in a leaf below)

Your Roots

Reflections on our family history, marriage, mothers, fathers, and faith

Here is our prayer for you as the newest member of our family tree (based on Ephesians 3:17-19).

I pray that you, being rooted and established in love, may have power together with all the saints, to grasp how wide and long and high and deep is the love of Christ, and to know this love that surpasses knowledge—that you may be filled to the measure of all the fullness of God. Amen!

Waiting for You

Waiting for you is a time of great anticipation, excitement, and wonder. It is a time of preparation. It is an "advent" of sorts.

Advent means "to come." As we prepare for the celebration of Christ's birth during the late fall and early winter, we nest, worship, and pray.

When we learned of your coming

_____
_____
_____
_____

How we told family and friends

_____
_____
_____
_____

The date we expected you was

_____

You were born on

_____

You arrived home on

_____

As an expectant parent,
the nesting begins!

Preparing a safe environment within the body and home

Resting, eating right, and keeping fit

Reading name books and parenting guides

Washing and organizing little clothes

Arranging the nursery with crib, rocking chair, and changing table

How we prepared the home

_____
_____
_____

Some of the books we read

_____
_____
_____

Your nursery furniture

_____
_____
_____

Some of your first clothes

_____
_____
_____

Kind words, gestures, and gifts from family, friends, and others

_____
_____
_____

Now is a time for prayer and reflection. Family members, friends, and our church family offer prayers for expectant parents, for siblings who will welcome a new brother or sister, and of course for the child who is about to join the family.

This is a time of wonder, hope, and a growing heart!

Your Name

What will we name you?

Finding the right name for you was so important. We spent a lot of time thinking about names while we waited for you!

There are many inspirations for baby names.

Grandparent names

Other family names

Names that begin with the same initial as a parent or other siblings

Biblical names

Names of people, places, or things that we like

PUMPKIN

Naming a child is a celebration of who we are in God's world
and who we hope our child will become in God's world.

Here are some names we considered for you!

_____

_____

_____

_____

_____

We decided on your name because

_____

_____

_____

_____

_____

Here are some nicknames we call you!

_____

_____

_____

_____

_____

Your Name _____

A good name is to be chosen rather than great riches. (Proverbs 22:1)

Every generous act of giving, with every perfect gift, is from above, coming down from the Father of lights. (James 1:17)

Attach a picture of baby and family

He will not let your foot be moved. (Psalm 121:3)

We are the clay, and you are our potter; we are all the work of your hand. (Isaiah 64:8)

Stamp your baby's footprint onto a piece of cardstock and attach it here

Stamp your baby's handprint onto a piece of cardstock and attach it here

Welcome, Baby!

Baby has arrived! Attach a baby announcement in the open space below.

Name _____ Date of Birth _____

Time of Birth _____ Place of Birth _____

Weight _____ Length _____

We praise God for you! We give thanks for

What we thought, said, and did when we first saw you

You look like

Your first visitors were

Firsts

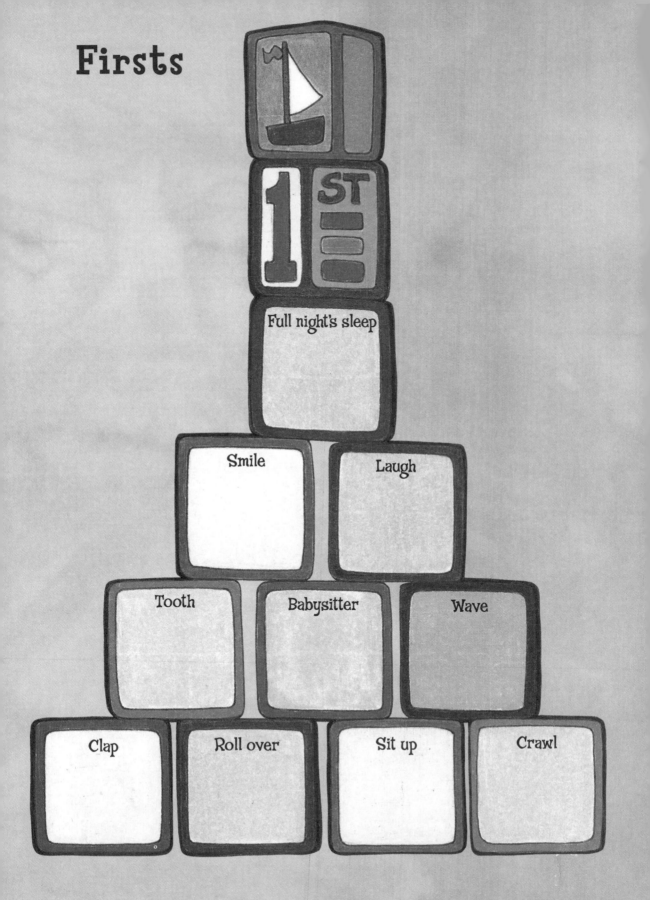

Here Are Some Other Firsts!

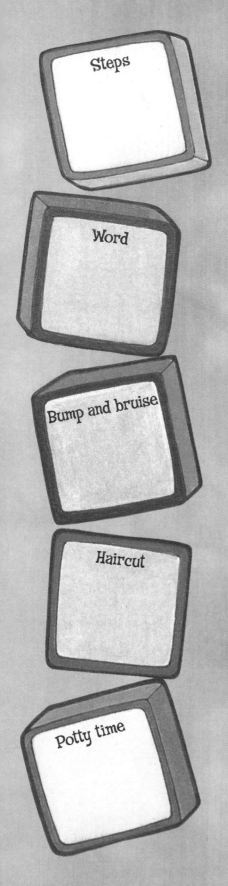

Steps

Word

Bump and bruise

Haircut

Potty time

_____
_____
_____
_____
_____
_____
_____
_____
_____
_____
_____
_____
_____
_____

God performs wonders that cannot be fathomed,
miracles that cannot be counted. (Job 5:9 NIV)

Our Favorites

A favorite outfit of yours

Attach a photo of child in outfit

A favorite face you make

A favorite place to go together

Attach a photo of child making a face

A favorite time of day with you

A favorite sound you make

Your Favorites

Your favorite music and songs

Your favorite snuggle pal

Your favorite play place

Your favorite snack

Your favorite friends

Your favorite Bible story

Your favorite storytelling spot

Your favorite books

Let the favor of the Lord our God
be upon us. (Psalm 90:17)

Getting to Know You

You communicate with us by

_____

_____

_____

On our good days

_____

_____

_____

On our difficult days

_____

_____

_____

What makes you

Laugh

Cry

Afraid

Sleepy

Attach a photo of child

I praise you, for I am fearfully and
wonderfully made. Wonderful are your
works; that I know very well. (Psalm 139:14)

The Many Faces of Baby

Choose an expression listed below and attach a photo of your baby showing it

Choose an expression listed below and attach a photo of your baby showing it

Sad

Happy

Content

Surprised

Playful

Mad

Sleepy

Serious

Choose an expression listed above and attach a photo of your baby showing it

Choose an expression listed above and attach a photo of your baby showing it

Baptism Is a Gift!

Those present
at the service of Baptism

Godparents

Date of Baptism

What Is Baptism?

In his *Small Catechism*, Martin Luther wrote "Baptism is not water alone, but it is water used together with God's Word and by God's command."

The words are "I baptize you in the name of the Father, and of the Son, and of the Holy Spirit."

The command is found in Matthew 28:19 when Jesus says, "Go therefore and make disciples of all nations, baptizing them in the name of the Father and of the Son and of the Holy Spirit."

At baptism, the word of God is made visible with water. The water symbolizes the cleansing hand of God in our lives. Jesus is present in the waters of baptism, washing us clean.

Each day the baptized are washed clean in the word of God through God's promise of love, forgiveness, and newness of life. What an astounding gift!

This gift should be "opened" as soon as possible. Infant baptism ensures that the gift of God's presence in our lives is available today!

Planning Your Child's Baptism

We baptize because we are commanded by God to do so. We are told to go forth and baptize all nations. In baptism God forgives sin, delivers from death and the devil, and gives everlasting salvation to all who believe. This is a great gift of grace from our God. This gift is to be given, opened, and enjoyed as soon as possible.

Planning for your child's baptismal day is exciting. It is a day of great joy, hope, and love. Where does one start? With prayer! Pray for your child. Pray as you choose your child's godparents. Pray that you will be emotionally and spiritually present during the event.

Then call your pastor and set up a meeting to discuss dates, times, and preparation. Some churches offer classes and great resources.

We set this baptismal date _____

We invited these people _____

We chose this outfit _____

Other ways we prepared for our child's baptism _____
_____

Here are some questions to ask your pastor:

 Where should the family sit during the service?

 Who will join the child at the font?

 Will another person be baptized at the same time?

 Can video and pictures be taken during the baptism?

 Can the family provide flowers for the altar or font?

 What if the baby cries?

Here are other baptismal traditions in our family:

_____

_____

_____

_____

_____

_____

_____

_____

Choosing Godparents

The tradition of a baptism sponsor or godparent is long standing. Many parents choose siblings or dear friends to hold this esteemed position on the day of the child's baptism. What a great honor to be asked to stand at the font with the child, parents, and clergy!

The choice for godparents may seem easy. Eldest brother and wife. Our closest sibling. The best man or maid of honor from our wedding. Dear, dear friends who have been with us through thick and thin. But the most important factor to consider while making this decision is their Christian faith. You are inviting the godparents to join you in raising your child in faith.

Here are some questions to consider when choosing godparents:

Do they actively participate in the life of a congregation?

Do they talk about their faith openly?

Do they read and study the Bible?

Are they prayerful?

Will they help you raise your child in faith?

Do they know that they will promise at the font to help you do so?

Will they commit to a lifelong relationship with your child?

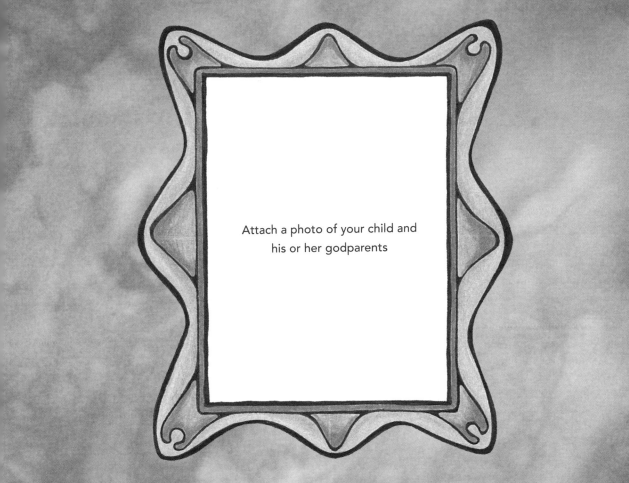

Attach a photo of your child and
his or her godparents

Names of your godparents _____

Special godparent moments _____

_____

_____

Special gifts from godparents _____

Mother's godparents _____

Father's godparents _____

Let love be genuine. Hold fast to what is good. Love one another with mutual affection; outdo one another in showing honor. Do not lag in zeal, be ardent in spirit, serve the Lord. (Romans 12:9-11)

Remembering Baptism

Celebrate God's promises!
God's promise of rebirth is
life-giving! God's promise
of renewal is energizing and
hope-filled!

Parents and godparents
make promises, too. At baptism
they promise to bring the child to
worship, share the word of God,
and pray for the child as they raise
him or her in faith. Celebrate the
promises you have made!

Attach a picture of your child
on his/her baptism day

We are born anew! As baptized members of God's family we are born anew each day! Martin Luther says this in his *Small Catechism*: "Our sinful self, with all its evil deeds and desires, should be drowned through daily repentance; and that day after day a new self should arise to live with God in righteousness and purity forever."

Write a prayer you can say every day as you make the sign of the cross on your child's forehead.

_____
_____
_____
_____
_____

Here is a ritual we use for remembering your baptism!

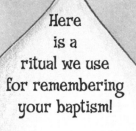

_____
_____
_____
_____

Remember baptism each day! Start by giving thanks to God each morning for a new day and a new beginning. Pray over your child and make the sign of the cross, just as your child was marked on the day of his or her baptism. As your child grows in years and wisdom, this ritual will remind her or him that we are made new in Christ.

Christmas Memories

This is what we want to remember about your first Christmas traditions, friends, family, food, gifts, happenings, and gatherings.

_____

_____

_____

_____

_____

_____

_____

_____

_____

_____

_____

I am bringing you good news of great joy for all the people: to you is born this day in the city of David a Savior, who is the Messiah, the Lord. (Luke 2:10-11)

Easter Reflections

This is what we want to remember about your first Easter traditions, friends, family, food, gifts, happenings, and gatherings.

_____
_____
_____
_____
_____
_____
_____
_____
_____
_____
_____

I know that you are looking for Jesus who was crucified.
He is not here; for he has been raised, as he said. (Matthew 28:5-6)

Worship Time

At worship, we sit near

_____

_____

You snuggle with

_____

_____

During the sermon, you

_____

_____

When we sing at worship, you

_____

_____

When we pray at worship, you

_____

_____

Our favorite Bible verses are

_____

_____

Attach a picture of your family
in front of your church

Jesus said to them, "Let the little children come to me; do not stop them; for it is to

In the Church Nursery

The first time you visited the church nursery, you

When we are in the church nursery, you

Attach a picture of your child and the caregiver in the nursery

Attach a picture of your child with pastor or other church members

You play with these friends

You enjoy these toys

You like these books

such as these that the kingdom of God belongs." (Mark 10:14)

Circles of Prayers

You like to pray for

A prayer you have memorized

You first said, "Amen"

Rejoice always, pray without ceasing, give thanks in all circumstances; for this is the will of God in Christ Jesus for you. (1 Thessalonians 5:16-18)

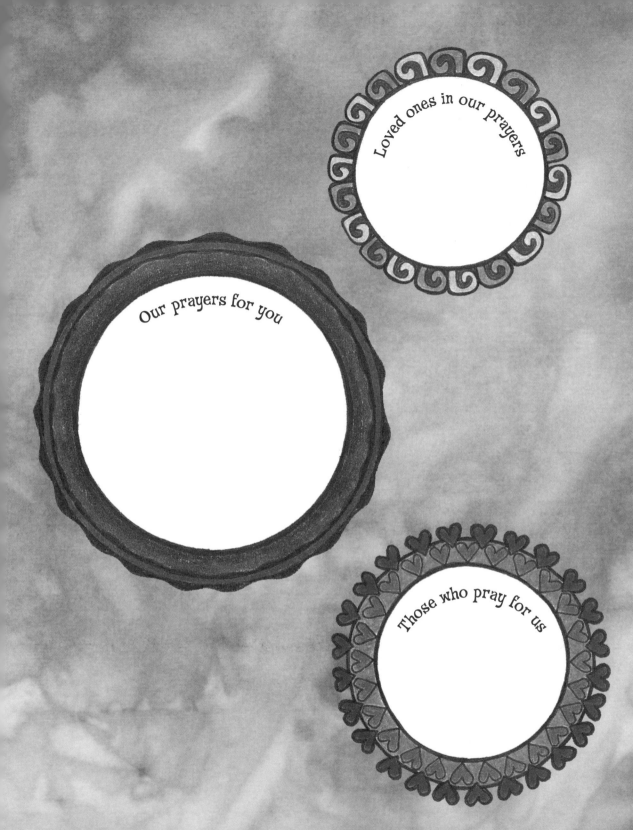

Loved ones in our prayers

Our prayers for you

Those who pray for us

When I remember you in my prayers, I always thank my God because I hear of your love for all the saints and your faith toward the Lord Jesus. (Philemon 1:4-5)

Attach a picture of your child in pajamas

What soothes you

Your favorite places to sleep

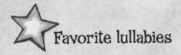
You snuggle with

Our sleepy time routine

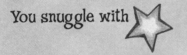
Favorite lullabies

Our bedtime prayers

Be at rest once more, O my soul,
for the Lord has been good to you.
(Psalm 116:7 NIV)

Bless This Mess

Our mealtime routine

_____

_____

_____

_____

_____

God is great, God is good,
Let us thank God for our food. Amen.
–Traditional table prayer

Your food and drink likes

_____

_____

_____

_____

Your food and drink dislikes

_____

_____

_____

_____

Favorite Recipes and Meals

Attach a picture of your child eating

Favorite breakfast

Favorite lunch

Favorite dinner

Games we play to get you to eat

_____
_____
_____
_____

Favorite table prayers

_____
_____
_____
_____

Favorite snack

Bath Time Fun!

Splish

Splash

Attach a picture of your child
during bath time

Rub a dub dub, who's in the tub?

When we put you in the water, you

_____

_____

_____

Our bath time routine looks like this

_____

_____

_____

Your favorite bath toys are

_____

_____

_____

After your bath, you smell like

_____

_____

_____

Soaps, shampoos, creams, and lotions we use

_____

_____

_____

Create in me a clean heart, O God, and
put a new and right spirit within me.
(Psalm 51:10)

First Birthday

Attach a photo of the birthday child's celebration

We celebrated by

_____

_____

_____

Who was there

_____

_____

_____

Our birthday prayer for you

_____

_____

_____

You are 1!

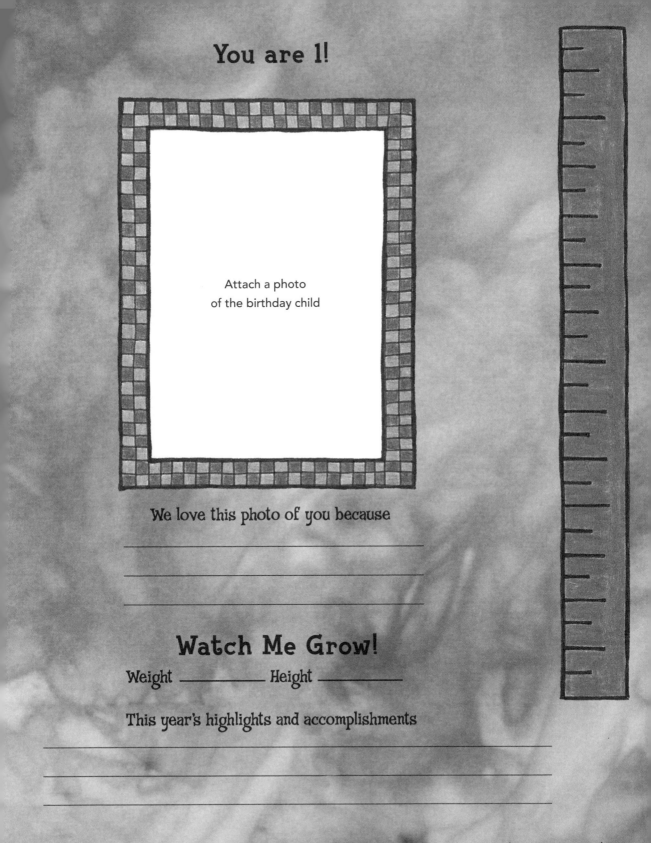

Attach a photo
of the birthday child

We love this photo of you because

_____

_____

_____

Watch Me Grow!

Weight _____ Height _____

This year's highlights and accomplishments

_____

_____

_____

This is the day that the Lord has made; let us rejoice and be glad in it. (Psalm 118:24)

First Baptism Birthday

What a special occasion to acknowledge in the life of your child! Baptism is much more then a white dress and a brunch. Baptism is a milestone in every Christian's life. Each baptism birthday is an occasion worth marking.

On the day marking your child's first baptismal birthday, start a tradition! Try something simple you can easily continue in the years ahead. The simplest thing to do is light a candle. You can use the candle lit during your child's service of baptism, but any candle will do. As you light the candle, say a prayer thanking God for the gift of forgiveness and renewal.

The next time you worship, go to the font at your church and mark your child (and yourself!) with the sign of the cross with the waters.

Remembering Your Baptism

This is what we remember about the day of your baptism.

Date _____

Time _____

Weather _____

_____

_____

Place _____

_____

_____

Special people present _____

_____

_____

How we spent the day

_____

_____

_____

_____

_____

_____

_____

_____

_____

Attach a photo of your child on this special day

Second Birthday

Attach a photo of the birthday child's celebration

We celebrated by

_____

_____

_____

Who was there

_____

_____

_____

Our birthday prayer for you

_____

_____

_____

You are 2!

Attach a photo
of the birthday child

We love this photo of you because

_____

_____

_____

Watch Me Grow!

Weight _____ Height _____

This year's highlights and accomplishments

_____

_____

_____

Grow in the grace and knowledge of our Lord and Savior Jesus Christ. To him be the glory both now and to the day of eternity. Amen (2 Peter 3:18)

Second Baptism Birthday

You may have started a baptismal tradition of marking your child with the cross each morning. You may have lit the baptismal candle on your child's first baptismal birthday. If not, you can still begin meaningful baptism traditions with your child!

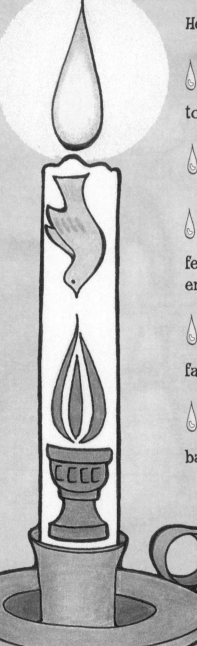

Here are some ideas:

Create a baptism photo book with pictures of your child's baptismal day. Look at them together and tell the story of his or her baptism.

Read from a Bible storybook about Jesus' baptism.

Check your church library and Christian bookstores for books about baptism. Read a few with your child to see which ones she or he enjoys.

Plan a baptism birthday party to celebrate this special day. Invite godparents and other faithful friends to attend.

Sing a song like "Jesus Loves Me" or "This Little Light of Mine" as you light your child's baptismal candle.

Arrange to donate altar flowers on the Sunday before her or his baptismal birthday.

Learn a new mealtime or bedtime prayer, or make one up together!

To reflect on your child's baptism, borrow a copy of the baptismal liturgy you used during the service. Read through the words again, and jot down some reflections.

In the service of baptism, we said this:

_____

Here is how we are keeping our promise:

_____

_____

_____

In the service of baptism, we said this:

_____

Here is how we are keeping our promise:

_____

_____

_____

_____

In the service of baptism, we said this:

_____

Here is how we are keeping our promise:

_____

_____

_____

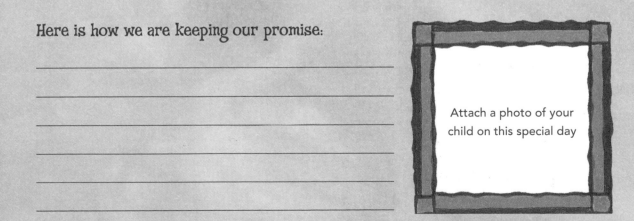

Attach a photo of your child on this special day

_____

_____

Third Birthday

Attach a photo of the birthday child's celebration

We celebrated by
_____
_____
_____

Who was there
_____
_____
_____

Our birthday prayer for you
_____
_____
_____

Your birthday wish
_____
_____
_____

3RD

2ND

1ST

You are 3!

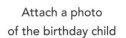

We love this photo of you because

_____

_____

_____

Watch Me Grow!

Weight _____ Height _____

This year's highlights and accomplishments

_____

_____

_____

The child grew and became strong, filled with wisdom;
and the favor of God was upon him. (Luke 2:40)

Third Baptism Birthday

Along with your child's date of birth, his or her baptism birthday should be on your calendar, too. Ask godparents and other special people in your child's life to remember this wonderful day with a card, phone call, or surprise visit.

For your child's third baptismal birthday, enjoy a baptism field trip together! Plan a time when you and your child can explore the baptismal font at your church. You could arrive early before worship, stay after the service, or ask your pastor if you could visit at another time.

On your field trip, try some of these things together:

- Splash around in the water in the font. Then make a little cross on each others' foreheads with your wet fingertips.

- Look for baptismal symbols like a shell and a dove.

- Point out the candle used for lighting the baptismal candle.

- Bring along a picture of the baptismal day. Show it to your child and point out how much your child has grown.

- Say a prayer together. Invite your child to pray for others in God's family.

- Finish your field trip together with a special snack like a treat with blue frosting or some blue gelatin.

Create a baptism story you can tell your child about the day. If you read it often enough, your child may memorize the story and share it with others!

_____ (Child's name), you are a child of God forever!

You were baptized on _____ (date of baptism).

The weather outside was _____ (describe the day's weather).

You were _____ (age of child at baptism) old when you were baptized.

You were baptized at _____ (name of church).

You wore _____ (describe child's baptismal outfit).

We chose _____ (godparents' names) as your godparents.

Many other special people were there too, like _____

_____ (name some of the people who attended).

When the pastor splashed you with baptism waters, you _____

_____ (describe how child responded).

After the service, we celebrated by _____

_____ (describe how your family celebrated).

You received some baptismal gifts, like _____

_____ (describe gifts).

On the day of your baptism we were so _____

_____

_____.

This is a prayer we can pray together:
Dear God, We're so glad to be part of your big
family! Thank you for the gift of baptism. Help us
remember your love for us. Amen

Attach a photo of your
child on this special day

Starting Sunday School

Dear Child of God,

You began learning about God's love for you since the time we knew you would be part of our family. We held you, fed you, talked to you, and kept you warm, dry, and safe. We prayed for you. We want our actions to show God's love flowing through us.

At baptism we promised to bring you to God's house, teach you God's commandments, and teach you to pray. Our church is God's house. People we meet in God's house are our church family!

When you begin Sunday school, you will meet more people in our church family. Sunday school will be a new experience for you! You will be in a familiar place, God's house, but we may not be there. We know you will have a good time meeting your teacher and new friends. We will pray for you!

Love,

Here are some ideas that will help your child prepare for and enjoy Sunday school:

✝ Ask if there is an orientation for young children where kids can see their room and meet their teachers. (If not, try to do this on your own!)

✝ Visit other rooms that kids may go to during Sunday school like the library and music room.

✝ Plan for your family to attend Christian education on a regular basis.

✝ Set out clothes the night before.

✝ Eat a good breakfast.

✝ Arrive early.

✝ Pray with your child about the new experience.

✝ Pray for your child's teachers and classmates.

✝ Learn what songs are played during Sunday school and sing them together.

✝ Visit the church library often and check out some books.

✝ Read and reread favorite stories from a Bible storybook.

✝ Be on time to pick up your child.

✝ Ask what happened in Sunday school.

✝ Post artwork and lessons on the fridge at home.

✝ Write a card of encouragement and thanks to your child's teacher.

Teach these words to your children talking about them when you are at home and when you are away, when you lie down and when you rise. Write them on the doorposts of your house and on your gates. (Deuteronomy 11:19-20)

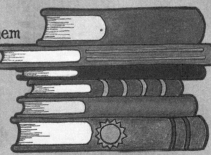

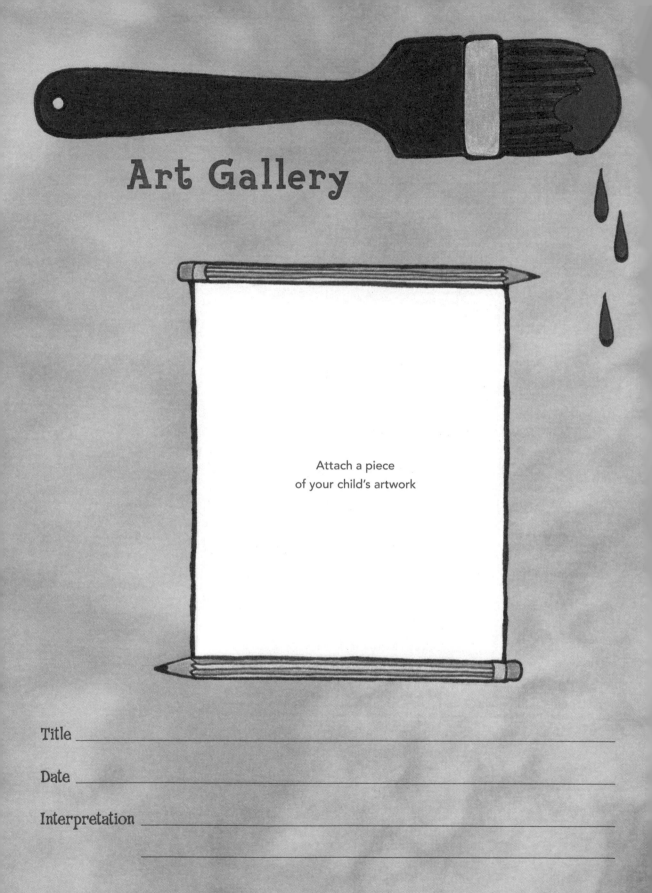

Art Gallery

Attach a piece
of your child's artwork

Title _____

Date _____

Interpretation _____

_____

Title _____

Date _____

Interpretation

_____

_____

_____

_____

_____

Attach a piece of your child's artwork

Attach a piece of your child's artwork

Title _____

Date _____

Interpretation

_____

_____

_____

_____

_____

_____

Art Gallery

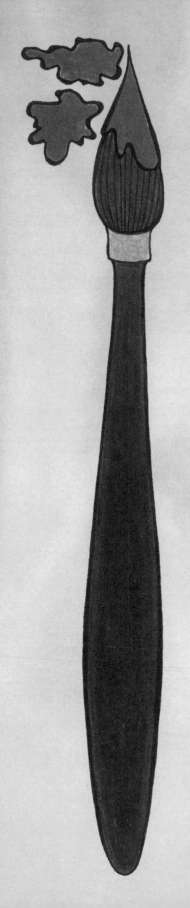

Attach a piece of your child's artwork

Title _____

Date _____

Interpretation

_____

_____

_____

_____

Title _____

Date _____

Interpretation

_____

_____

_____

_____

Attach a piece of your child's artwork

The Lord is the everlasting God, the Creator of the ends of the earth. (Isaiah 40:28)

Animals, Animals!

Some of your favorite stuffed animals and animal toys

_____

_____

_____

_____

_____

Some pets you enjoy

_____

_____

_____

_____

_____

_____

Here are some animal sounds you make!

Dog   Cat

Pig   Cow

Horse   Lamb

Bird   Lion

What you like about the story of Noah's Ark

_____

_____

_____

_____

_____

_____

Other favorite Bible stories about animals

_____

_____

_____

_____

_____

_____

O Lord, the earth is full of your creatures. (Psalm 104:24)

Love Letters

Dear Parents, Godparents, Grandparents, and Special Someones,

Please write a letter to me. Share your hopes and prayers, fears and worries, sources of strength and inspiration, and musings on yourself and your relationship with me. Include a favorite photo of us together.

Love,
Me!

Note to Parents: Purchase a stationery set and distribute the cards and envelopes to loved ones in your child's life. Attach their response to these pages or in another special place.

Musings

Inspiration

Joys

Fears

Worries

Prayers

Hopes

Faith

Strength

Reflections

Friends

Family

I have indeed received much joy and encouragement from your love . . . (Philemon 1:7)

Love Letters

A Morning Prayer

Dear God,
Thank you for the sun.
Thank you for my breakfast.
Thank you for my family.
Thank you for the day ahead.
Amen

Prayers

Bedtime Prayer

Dear Jesus,
Now I go to bed,
On my pillow I rest my head.
I know you'll bless me all the night!
I will wake with the sun so bright!
Amen

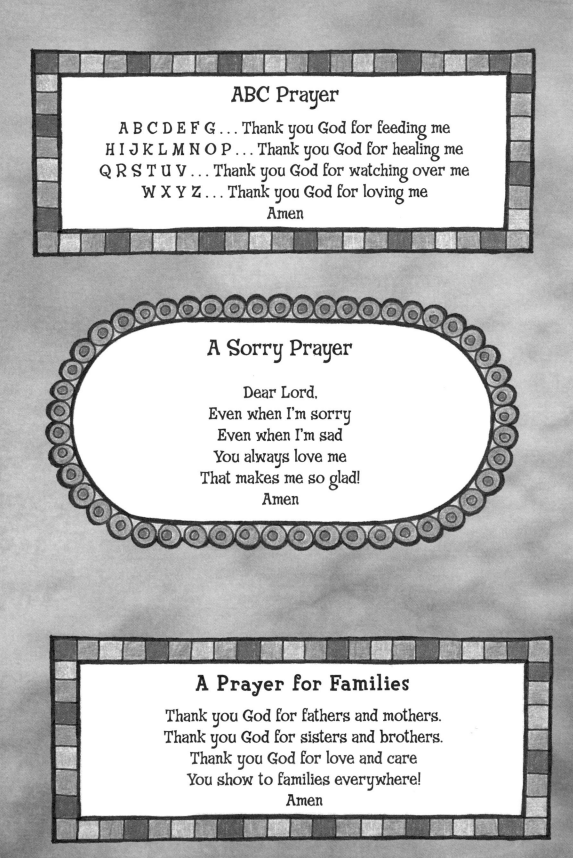

ABC Prayer

A B C D E F G ... Thank you God for feeding me
H I J K L M N O P ... Thank you God for healing me
Q R S T U V ... Thank you God for watching over me
W X Y Z ... Thank you God for loving me
Amen

A Sorry Prayer

Dear Lord,
Even when I'm sorry
Even when I'm sad
You always love me
That makes me so glad!
Amen

A Prayer for Families

Thank you God for fathers and mothers.
Thank you God for sisters and brothers.
Thank you God for love and care
You show to families everywhere!
Amen

Final Words

Use this page to write any other reflections and thoughts
on the faith formation of your child.

_____

_____

_____

_____

_____

_____

_____

_____

_____

_____

_____

_____

_____

_____

_____

_____

_____

_____

_____

_____